Pretty Gifts

Things to Make and Do

Bath • New York • Singapore • Hong Kong • Cologne • Delhi
Melbourne • Amsterdam • Johannesburg • Auckland • Shenzhen

This edition published by Parragon in 2011

Parragon
Queen Street House
4 Queen Street
Bath BA1 1HE, UK

ISBN 978-1-4454-1808-7
Printed in China.

Contents

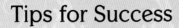

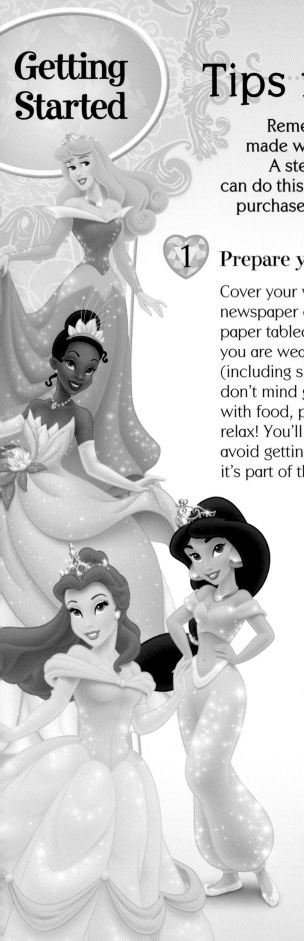

Tips for Success

Remember, everything in this book should be made with the supervision and help of a grown up! A step labeled with "Kids" means that a child can do this step on their own. Some items will need to be purchased from a supermarket or a craft/hobby store.

1 Prepare your space

Cover your workspace with newspaper or a plastic or paper tablecloth. Make sure you are wearing clothes (including shoes!) that you don't mind getting splattered with food, paint or glue. But relax! You'll never completely avoid getting messy; in fact, it's part of the fun!

2 Wash your hands

Wash your hands before starting a new project, and clean up as you go along. Clean hands make for clean crafts! Remember to wash your hands afterwards too, using soap and warm water to remove any of the remaining materials.

3 Follow steps carefully

Follow each step carefully, and in the order in which it appears. We've tested all the projects; we know they work, and we want them to work for you, too.

4 Measure precisely

If a project gives you measurements, use your ruler, measuring cups, or measuring spoons to make sure you measure as accurately as you can. Sometimes, the success of the project may depend on it.

5 Be patient

You may need to wait while something bakes, and leave paint, glue or clay to dry, sometimes for a few hours or even overnight. Be patient! Plan another activity while you wait, but it's important not to rush something as it may affect the outcome!

6 Clean up

When you've finished your project, clean up any mess. Store all the materials together so that they are ready for the next time you want to make and do. If you are making something with someone else then ensure it is a team effort!

Pretty Paw Prints

Your pets deserve the best so make them a wonderful jar to keep their most special treats in!

1

Stick some strips of double-sided tape onto both sheets of colored card. Cut out eight circles, four pink and four blue from the card.

You will need

- A large empty jar with a lid
- Colored card stock – 2 sheets in 2 colors e.g. pink & blue
- Double-sided tape
- Safety scissors
- Glue and paintbrush

2

On the remaining card, draw the paw shapes. Make four blue and four pink. Each paw will consist of a curvy heart shape for the centre and four small ovals. Cut out each paw print.

Kids 3

Glue the paw print patterns onto the card circles. Then peel off the tape from the back of the circles and stick onto the jar. You should have pink on blue and vice versa.

Snow White's tip:
If you don't like paw prints you could try other shapes, such as hearts!

Sock Mice Friends

The mice are Cinderella's bestest friends.
Now make your own friends cute mice
to play with!

Kids

1

Stuff some cotton balls into the toe
end of the sock so it is about one
third full.

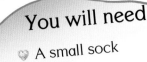

You will need

- A small sock
- Safety scissors
- Yarn
- Cotton balls
- Felt
- Fabric glue
- Ribbon for tail

2

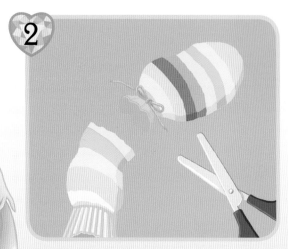

Tie up the end of the sock with a
long piece of wool then trim off the
open end.

3

Cut two felt circles (approx. 1½
inches in diameter). Add glue
to one edge of the circles and then
pinch the edges together into ear
shapes. Allow to dry.

4

Cut small felt circles for the eyes and glue them onto the sock along with the ears and yarn whiskers. Glue a ribbon on for the tail.

Cinderella's tip:
Your friends can place their mice on their neatly made beds! They look so cute!

Floral Tea Set

Every princess loves to host a tea party with their friends. Now you can make your own petal decorated tea set to use over and over again.

You will need

- A plain plate, cup, and saucer—washed and dried
- Ceramic paints
- Markers
- Craft foam
- Cotton swab or thin felt pen
- Paint brush

Kids

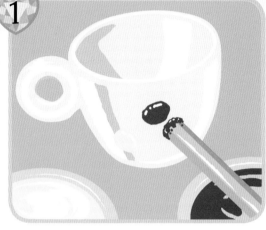

1

Firstly ensure the tea set has been approved by a grown up for decorating! Then dip the end of a marker into paint and print circles onto the cups and saucers.

2

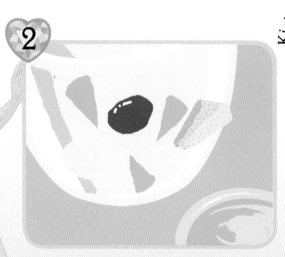

Cut out leaf shapes from the craft foam. These are small triangles. These will be your printing pieces. Dip in green paint and add to your tea set.

Kids

3

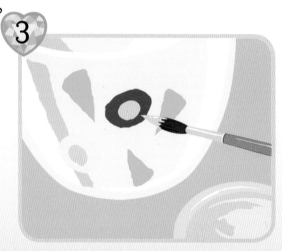

When the paint is dry, add smaller dots using the end of a thin pen, cotton swab or paint brush, in the centre of the circles.

Happy Easter!

© Mattel

© Mattel

© Mattel

© Mattel

Fab CHICK!
Barbie

© Mattel

© Mattel

© Mattel

© Mattel

© Mattel

I ♥ Easter

© Mattel

© Mattel

© Mattel

Happy Easter!

© Mattel

© Mattel

Barbie

© Mattel

© Mattel

Happy Easter!

Belle's tip:
Throw someone a tea
party. Pour in apple juice
and pretend
it's tea!

Brush a lighter green line onto each leaf shape. Allow to dry. Then host a tea party!

Ariel

Shell Jewelry Box

Ariel keeps her most precious things safe inside a shell box. These make wonderful gift boxes or as a present on their own.

You will need

- A cardboard container with lid
- 2 sheets of red felt
- Pencil
- Safety scissors
- White glue and brush
- Blue acrylic paint and brush
- Assorted seashells

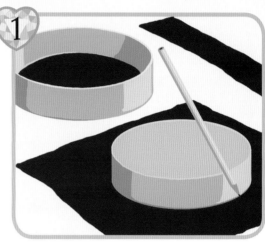

1 Trace around the lid of the box onto the red felt. Cut it out, and stick it inside the lid. Repeat, and stick into the inside bottom of the box.

2 Measure the depth of the box and cut a long strip of felt the same width. Glue it around the inside of the box. Trim the ends to make it fit neatly. Let dry.

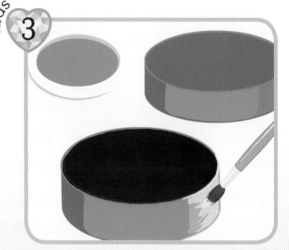

3 Paint the outside and base of both the lid and box with the blue acrylic paint.

4

Arrange the shells on the box lid and glue them on.

5

Smaller boxes can be decorated with a single shell. Use them as gift boxes for earrings and rings.

Ariel's tip:
Seashells are the homes of creatures called shellfish. Once the animal has gone, you can use the shells for all sorts of crafts.

Palace Invitations

Whether you're hosting a tea party or a big birthday bash, sending personal handmade invites to your friends is always something special!

You will need

- Colored card stock in 2 shades of blue, light and dark
- Paper in gold, silver, and purple
- White glue
- Scissors
- Sequins, gems, sequins or sticky stars

1

Cut out a rectangular card shape from the light blue card. Fold in half. Stick a slightly smaller dark blue rectangular card to the front of the larger piece.

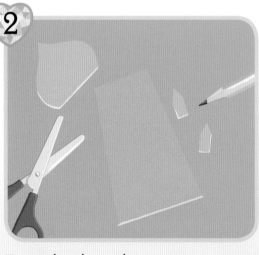

2

To make the palace tower cut out a tall rectangular shape from the purple paper. Then cut out an onion shape from the gold paper to go on top.

3

Stick the shapes onto the background. Allow the glue to dry. Cut out a moon shape from the silver paper.

Add stars and sequins using glue. Glue on your moon. Allow to dry then write your party invitation message on the front/inside of the card.

Jasmine's tip:
You can use glitter and glue to make a starry night sky.

Jasmine's Palace Party

Ariel

Shimmering Fish

These fabulous fish are pretty and shimmer just like they do under the ocean. Give some to a friend so they can put them up in a window and watch them shine!

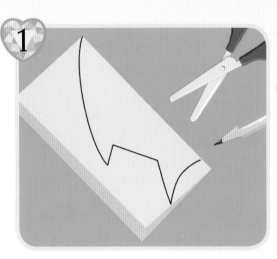

1

Fold a piece of card 15½ x 11½ inches in half. Draw half a fish shape then cut it out so you have a fish shaped template.

You will need
- Card (cut from a cereal box)
- Pencil
- Scissors
- Aluminium foil
- Colored candy wrappers
- Glue
- Brush
- White card stock
- Felt pen
- Thread and tape to hang up

2

Place the template onto card stock and draw around the edge. Cut it out. You can use the template to make more fish shapes.

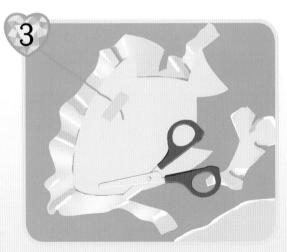

3

Cut two pieces of foil roughly the same size as the fish. Crinkle the foil then paste onto both sides. Press over the foil to stick it down, then trim around the edges.

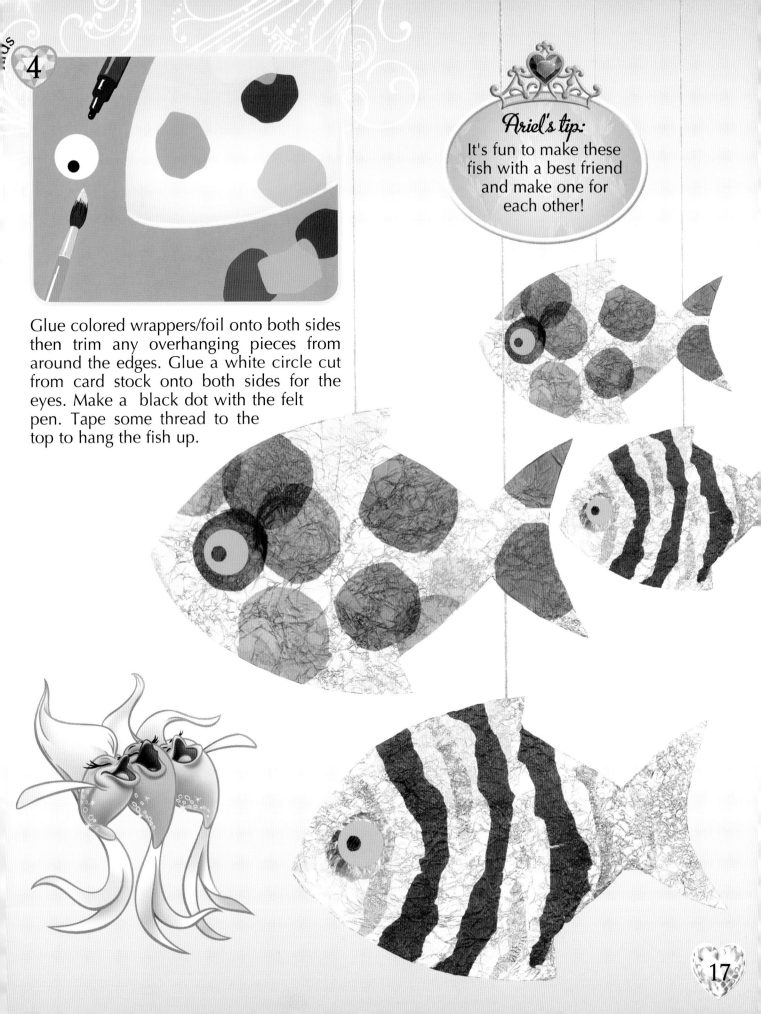

It's fun to make these
fish with a best friend
and make one for
each other!

Glue colored wrappers/foil onto both sides
then trim any overhanging pieces from
around the edges. Glue a white circle cut
from card stock onto both sides for the
eyes. Make a black dot with the felt
pen. Tape some thread to the
top to hang the fish up.

Aurora Beautiful Bath Salts

These lovely bath salts add style to the bathroom and smell sweet every bath time!

You will need

- Small gift jars with tight fitting lids
- Epsom salts – enough to fill the jars
- Food coloring
- Small bowls or plastic containers
- Spoons
- A few drops of scented oil
- Ribbon – 11½ inches for each jar and a plastic gem
- Glue

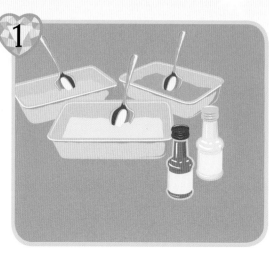

1 Divide the Epsom salts equally into three plastic containers or bowls. Add a few drops of food coloring and scented oil to each cup. Mix with a spoon. The colors should be pale and pretty.

2 Carefully spoon the first color into the jars. Press the salt down as you go so it is packed tight. Drop your scented oil onto the top.

3 Using separate spoons for each color add the other colored salts to make a striped pattern in the jars, adding a few drops of scented oil to each layer.

Aurora's tip:
Make these for
your friends in their
favorite colors!

Put the lids firmly onto the jars. Tie ribbons around the top with a dot of glue to keep it in place. Glue a sparkly gem to the middle.

Pet Photo Frame

If you know someone who likes animals as much as Jasmine does, then make this cute frame for your friends or family to show off their favorite pet or animal.

You will need

- 4 cardboard strips 6 x 1 inches
- 12 ice cream sticks
- Cardboard (to fit photo)
- 2 different-sized pens (any kind)
- Acrylic paints
- Scissors
- Clear adhesive tape

Kids

1

Paint the sticks and let dry.

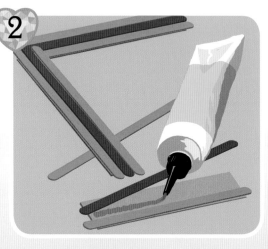

2

Glue three sticks onto each cardboard strip, leaving about an inch gap at both ends. Then glue the ends of the cardboard strips together into a frame shape.

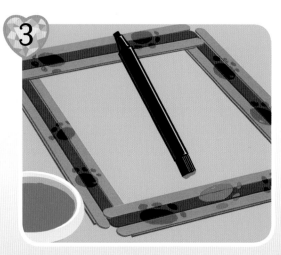

3

Dip the end of the largest pen into the paint and press down around the frame. Then use the smaller pen to add circles to complete the paw prints.

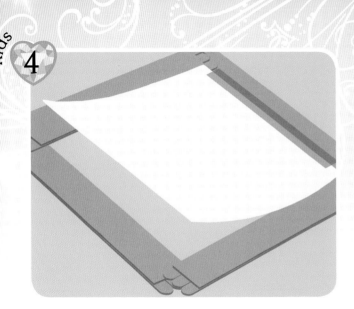

Jasmine's tip: Your friends or family can place their new photo frame by their bedside!

Tape a photo of your pet into the frame then cover the back with a piece of cardboard.

Cinderella Bubble Gift Wrap

Now it's time to make some bubbly gift wrap with Cinderella. It's so much fun! Why don't you give it a try?

You will need

- Old newspapers
- Acrylic paints: purple, yellow
- Dish washing liquid
- Water
- Old spoon
- Drinking straws
- Shallow bowl
- White paper
- Measuring spoons and cups

1

Cover your work surface with newspaper. Using a spoon, stir together ½ cup of water, 1 or 2 tablespoons purple paint, and ½ tablespoon dish washing liquid in the bowl.

2 Kids

Place a straw in the paint mixture and gently blow to make bubbles. Keep blowing until the bubbles are almost at the edge of the dish.

3 Kids

Put a piece of paper on top of the bubbles and hold it there until several bubbles have popped. Move the paper and continue popping bubbles until most of the paper has been painted. Don't push the paper too far into the bowl.

4

Clean the bowl and make a yellow paint mixture. Repeat steps 1 to 3 so you have a purple and yellow bubbly pattern on the piece of paper. Let dry before using the paper. Try different colors next time!

Cinderella's tip:
Use more dish washing liquid if you want to make more bubbles.

Enchanting Envelopes

These beautiful princess-inspired envelopes are perfect for sending your party invites. Or for mailing your best friend a letter!

You will need

- Sheet of 8½ x 11 inch colored paper
- Safety scissors
- Patterned gift wrap
- Glue stick
- A card sized template

Kids

1

Put your card template on the sheet of colored paper. Fold the paper in on two sides and the bottom. Then fold over the top of the paper to make the flap.

2

Unfold the paper and cut out the four small corner rectangles.

3

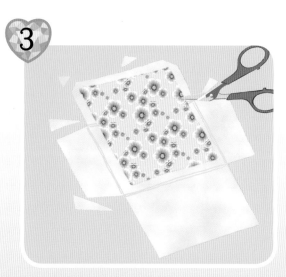

Cut a piece of gift wrap to fit in the top flap and main area. Leave ½ inch gap around the edge of the gift wrap. Glue in place. Trim the corners of the top and side flaps.

4

5

The Beast

Fold up the bottom flap, then fold in the sides and glue them in place. Place the homemade card inside, then fold down and glue the top flap.

You also can make a colorful envelope from patterned paper. Don't forget to add a label with the name of the person you're giving the card to on the front.

Belle's tip:
You can also add colorful stickers to decorate your envelope or to seal them!

Tiana

Flower Candies

Tiana loves to make scrumptious treats for all her friends. You might need a helping hand to make them, but certainly not eating them. Delicious!

You will need

To make 20 candies:
- 1 cup (225g) powdered sugar
- 1 egg white
- Juice of half a lemon
- A few drops of peppermint extract
- Green food coloring
- Bar of chocolate
- Sifter, bowl, cookie cutter, wooden spoon, saucepan

Kids

1

Sift the powdered sugar into a large mixing bowl.

2

Separate the egg yolk from the white. Add the egg white to the powdered sugar.

3

With your hands or a spoon, mix it together until you have made a soft dough. Add the lemon juice, peppermint extract and food coloring.

4

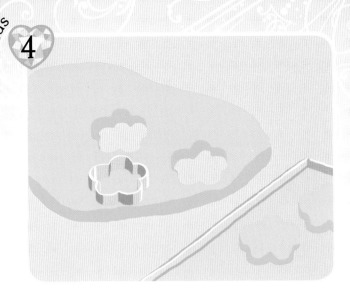

5

Pour the dough onto a cold surface and flatten it to about ½ inch thick. With a cookie cutter, cut out the shapes, put them on a baking sheet, and leave them in a cool, dry place to set for around 30 minutes.

Break up the bar of chocolate and put it in a bowl. Put the bowl over a saucepan of simmering water and stir the chocolate until it has melted.

Tiana's tip:
You could make fruit chocs instead. Dip strawberries, cherries, and sliced apple in the melted chocolate.

6

Take the bowl off the heat and quickly dip half of each candy into the chocolate. Leave the candies until the chocolate hardens.

27

Belle *Heart Diary*

Belle records all her most precious secrets, memories, and ideas in a diary and writes in it every day. A hand decorated diary makes for a very special present.

Kids

1

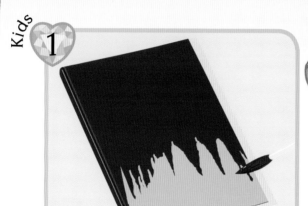

Place a piece of paper inside the front and back cover of the notebook, to stop the pages getting paint on them. Paint the entire notebook, then let it dry.

You will need

- A small plain hardcover notebook or diary
- 2 sheets of plain paper
- Paint
- Brushes
- Gold card stock
- Gemstone
- String
- White glue
- Ribbon

2

Cut four triangles of gold card and glue them to the corners of the notebook. Cut a heart shape from gold card and stick in the center of the cover.

Kids

3

Glue a gemstone in the middle. Make a curly pattern with glue then stick the string down over the top. Press it down. Glue red felt strips around the spine of the book.

Belle's tip:
This would make a wonderful present for your mom, grandma, or best friend!

Stick a ribbon to the inside back cover at the top of the page. This can be used as a bookmark. Now write inside your diary about your day, favorite things and pretty fashion ideas!

Ariel

Precious Purse

This precious purse is perfect for keeping your coins and treasures safe. Make one for someone you treasure!

You will need

- Cloth that won't fray
- 20 inches cord, ribbon, or wool
- 1 large bead
- Large plate and small plate
- Felt tip pen
- Scissors
- Colored card stock
- Buttons or beads

Kids

1

Put the cloth face down. Trace around a large plate onto the wrong side of the cloth. Then using a smaller plate, draw another circle on to the cloth in the center of the larger circle.

2

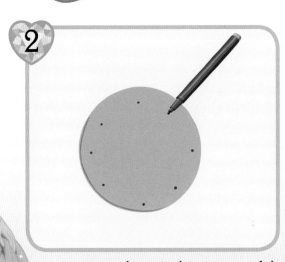

Cut out the circle. Use a felt tip pen to mark dots at 12, 3, 6 and 9 o'clock around the inner circle. Make dots inbetween these. Mark 8 more dots in between so that you have 16 dots altogether. Cut a tiny slit on each dot.

3

Draw and cut out a heart shape from colored card stock. Decorate the card and make a small hole near the top.

4

Thread the wool it in and out of the slits, slipping the heart on after the fourth slit.

5

Thread both ends of the cord through a large bead or button and knot the ends together. Now you are ready to decorate your purse and give it to someone special!

Ariel's tip:
Decorate your purse with sequins, beads, or stick-on jewels.

Aurora Pressed-flower Card

Pressed flowers can be used to make beautiful greeting cards. Don't forget to check with an adult before you pick flowers!

You will need

- Flowers and leaves
- Heavy books (e.g. dictionaries)
- Paper towels
- White glue mixed with equal amount of water, and brush
- Cream cardboard 16 x 18 inches
- Safety scissors and ruler

Kids **1**

Pick some flower petals and leaves. Arrange them on paper towels, then put another piece of paper towel on top. Place them inside a book. Place a pile of heavy books on top of the book with the flower, petals, and leaves inside. Leave them for at least two weeks to dry out.

Kids **2**

Fold the cream cardboard in half and make a sharp crease. Remove the pressed petals and leaves from the book. Arrange them on the front of the card and glue them in position.